Fannie Lou Hamer

Terry Barber

ACTS OF
COURAGE
SERIES

Fannie Lou Hamer is published by
Grass Roots Press, a division of Literacy Services of Canada Ltd.

PHONE 1–888–303–3213
WEBSITE www.grassrootsbooks.net

ACKNOWLEDGMENTS

We acknowledge the financial support of the Government of Canada through the Book Publishing Industry Development Program (BPIDP) for our publishing activities.

We acknowledge the support of
the Alberta Foundation for the Arts
for our publishing programs.

Editor: Dr. Pat Campbell
Image research: Dr. Pat Campbell
Book design: Lara Minja, Lime Design Inc.

Library and Archives Canada Cataloguing in Publication

Barber, Terry, date
    Fannie Lou Hamer / Terry Barber.

ISBN 978-1-894593-84-7

    1. Hamer, Fannie Lou. 2. Civil rights movements—United States—History—20th century. 3. African American women civil rights workers—Mississippi—Biography. 4. Civil rights workers—United States—Biography. 5. Readers for new literates. I. Title.

PE1126.N43B36362 2008   428.6'2   C2008-901985-7

Printed in Canada

Contents

Civil War battle.

The Civil War

It is 1861. The United States goes to war. The North fights the South. The states in the South believe in slavery. The states in the North **ban** slavery. The Civil War ends in 1865. The North wins. This war ends slavery.

Before the Civil War, slavery is legal in 15 states.

These people march for civil rights.

Life in the South

Fannie Lou Hamer is born in 1917. She grows up in the South. Black people are still not free. Black people are treated like second-class citizens. Black people do not have the same rights as white people.

Fannie Lou and her family live in Mississippi.

Jim Crow laws support segregation on buses.

Life in the South

The South has laws that keep black
and white people apart. They cannot
go to the same school. They cannot eat
together. They cannot sit together on
a bus. These laws support **segregation.**
These laws are called **Jim Crow.**

Jim Crow Laws

These laws segregate
black and white
people.

People must pass a literacy test before they register to vote.

Life in the South

Black people have the right to vote. But it is not easy to vote. People must register to vote. They must pass a literacy test. In the South, some white people hurt black voters. Many black people are afraid to vote.

The U.S. Constitution allows black people to vote in 1870.

This sharecropper picks cotton.

Life as a Sharecropper

Fannie Lou's parents are **sharecroppers**. They grow cotton on a farmer's land. The farmer gives them a share of the crop. The farmer sells them supplies. He charges high prices. Fannie Lou's parents are always in debt.

Fannie Lou Hamer is born on October 6, 1917.

A farmer sells supplies to sharecroppers.

A tar paper shack.

Life as a Sharecropper

Sharecropper is just another word for slave. Sharecroppers are born poor. They live and die poor. Fannie Lou's family live in a tar paper shack. They are often hungry. Their clothes are rags. They do not own shoes. They tie rags on their feet in place of shoes.

Fannie Lou has 14 brothers and 5 sisters.

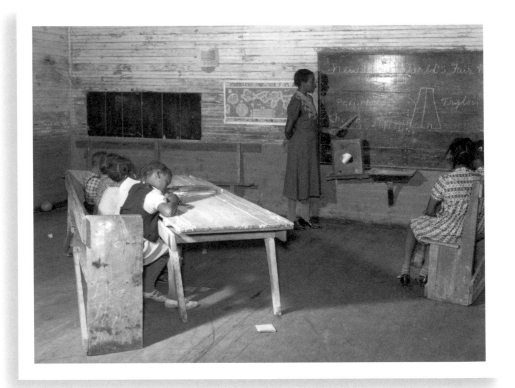

A Mississippi school.

Life as a Sharecropper

Fannie starts to pick cotton at the age of six. She works from dawn to **dusk**. She spends more time in the fields than in school. But, she learns to read and write. Fannie Lou has to quit school after Grade six.

A young girl picks cotton.

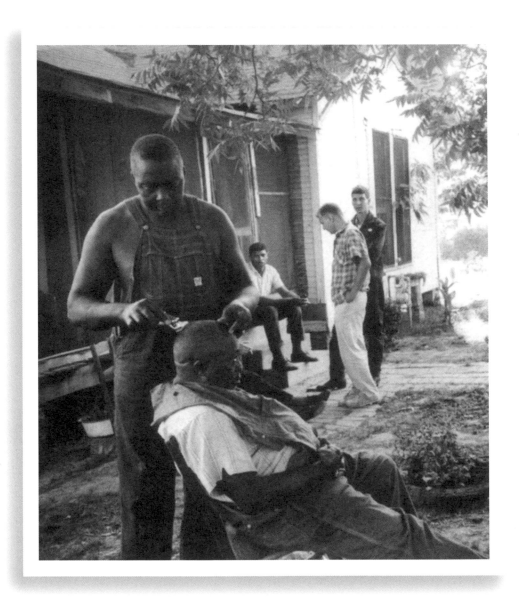

Perry Hamer trims a friend's hair.

Life as a Sharecropper

Fannie Lou marries a sharecropper. His name is Perry Hamer. They work on the same farm for 18 years. A white farmer owns the land. Fannie Lou works in the fields all day. She cleans the land-owner's house at night.

Fannie Lou marries Perry Hamer in 1944.

A church meeting about voter registration.

Act of Courage

In 1962, Fannie Lou goes to a church meeting. Black leaders make a speech. "Is anyone willing to vote?" they ask. "Please raise your hand." Fannie Lou is not scared to vote. She raises her hand. So do 17 other black people.

Police get ready to stop a bus.

Act of Courage

The group takes a bus to town. They
try to register to vote. They fail the
literacy test. The police stop them on
the way home. The police say, "Your
bus is too yellow." The police arrest
the bus driver.

Fannie Lou leaves her home.

Act of Courage

Fannie Lou arrives home. She hears some bad news. The land-owner is angry. He does not want black people to vote. He tells Fannie Lou to get off his land. She leaves her home. She leaves her family. She leaves her job.

A bullet hole in the window.

Act of Courage

Many white people are angry with
Fannie Lou. Some men want to kill
her. Fannie Lou stays with friends.
They live in Ruleville. One night, shots
are fired into the house. No one is
hurt.

Perry
Hamer joins
Fannie Lou after
harvest.

Fannie Lou lives in Ruleville, Mississippi.

Act of Courage

Fannie Lou leaves the town. She goes into hiding. Then she has a **change of heart**. Fannie Lou says, "I'm not a criminal… I got a right to live in Ruleville." She does not back down. Fannie Lou is brave.

People wait in line for voter registration.

Civil Rights Worker

Fannie Lou keeps trying to register to vote. She finally passes the literacy test. Fannie Lou becomes a civil rights worker. She wants black people to vote. She works hard to register black voters. She holds meetings. She makes speeches.

Fannie Lou passes the literacy test on January 10, 1963.

Civil rights workers see the police.

Civil Rights Worker

June 3, 1963 is an ugly day for Fannie
Lou. She is on a bus with other civil
rights workers. Police stop the bus.
The police know the people on the
bus want to register black voters.
The police take the people on the bus
to jail.

Fannie Lou spends three days in a jail cell.

Civil Rights Worker

Fannie Lou is taken to a cell. She is told to lie face down. The police say, "We are going to make you wish you was dead." Fannie Lou is badly beaten. After three days, the police let her go.

Fannie Lou Hamer makes a speech in 1965.

Civil Rights Worker

Fannie Lou keeps working to register voters. She gives speeches about voting rights. Her speeches give people hope. She says, "I am sick and tired of being sick and tired." Fannie Lou wants black people to have better lives.

Fannie Lou speaks at the Democratic National Convention.

Civil Rights Worker

Fannie Lou gives a speech in 1964. It is an election year. Fannie Lou talks about why blacks find it hard to vote. Many people see Fannie Lou on TV. Her speech leads to change.

Fannie Lou joins the Mississippi Freedom Democratic Party in 1964.

Lyndon B. Johnson is the U.S. President from 1963 to 1969.

U.S. President Johnson

New Laws

The South begins to change. Black people get more rights. In 1964, the U.S. President signs the Civil Rights Act. This law says that segregation is not legal. Now black and white people can use the same public places.

President Johnson signs the Civil Rights Act. July 2, 1964

A black person fills out a voter registration form.
Mississippi, 1965

New Laws

In 1965, the U.S. President signs the
Voting Rights Act. This law makes
it easier for black people to vote.
Black people are a step closer to real
freedom. This law is passed 100 years
after slavery ends.

Fannie Lou Hamer, 1964.

A Woman of Courage

Fannie Lou Hamer dies in 1977. People remember her as a brave woman. People remember her for risking her life for equal rights. Her work makes life better for black people. Now black people can vote without fear.

Glossary

ban: an official order that forbids something.

change of heart: to change one's feelings, attitude, or opinion.

dusk: time of day that follows sunset.

Jim Crow laws: these laws make segregation a legal act. For example, black and white people cannot use the same waiting room, school, or water fountain.

segregation: the act of separating a race or class from the rest of society.

sharecropper: a person who farms another's land for a share of the crop or profit.

Talking About the Book

What did you learn about Fannie Lou Hamer?

What words would you use to describe
Fannie Lou?

What did you learn about civil rights
in the U.S?

What was the purpose of the voter's literacy
test?

Fannie Lou says: "I am sick and tired of being
sick and tired." What does she mean?

Describe Fannie Lou's acts of courage.

Picture Credits